Nuts'nBolts
LEADERSHIP

"How To" Strategies and Practical Tips For Leaders at ALL Levels

Eric Harvey   Paul Sims

WALKTHETALK.COM

Resources for Personal and Professional Success

*Helping Individuals and Organizations Achieve Success
Through Values-Based Practices*

To order additional copies of this handbook or for information on
other WALK THE TALK® products and services,
contact us at
1.888.822.9255
or visit our website at
www.walkthetalk.com

Nuts'nBolts LEADERSHIP

Inquiries regarding permission for use of the material contained in this book should be addressed to:
The WALK THE TALK Company
1100 Parker Square, Suite 250
Flower Mound, Texas 75028
972.899.8300

WALK THE TALK books may be purchased for educational, business, or sales promotion use.

WALK THE TALK® and The WALK THE TALK® Company are registered trademarks of Performance
Systems Corporation.

Printed in the United States of America
10 9 8 7 6 5

Printed by MultiAd

ISBN 1-885228-48-1

9 781885 228482

90000

Introduction

We've been asked on more than a few occasions what we feel is the secret to leadership survival and success in today's challenging business world. And our answer is always the same:

Fewer long-winded theories and philosophies – more proven strategies and techniques!

If you've been in management for any length of time, you've undoubtedly come to realize that it's a multi-faceted profession – a somewhat complex calling that includes the classic and academically-described duties of "planning, directing, controlling, etc." … and much more.

Like a coin, leadership has two sides. There's the *proactive* side – the actions you initiate to positively affect people and their performance. And there's the *reactive* side – the actions you take in response to unanticipated issues and situations. The key to these equally-important sides is ACTION. And the way we see it, in order to act properly and effectively in these fast-paced times, your management "toolbox" needs to be filled with solid *nuts and bolts* techniques. That's precisely what this handbook is all about!

In the pages that follow, you'll find practical, easy-to-follow "how to's" to help you hone your skills and meet many of your most challenging leadership responsibilities. From motivating employees, communicating more effectively, and handling employee performance problems – to maximizing your time, hiring the best and brightest people, and molding an ethical and high-performing organization – we've attempted to *de*mystify the process of leadership by providing the guidance you need to survive and, more importantly, succeed.

USE and APPLY the information in this handbook, and you'll not only improve your overall effectiveness, but you'll also build a reputation (and a legacy) as a top-notch leader.

Contents

How To ...

Get Your Employees Fired-Up To Achieve

When individuals and teams are motivated, extraordinary things happen. The group seems to be on fire. Employees don't simply perform their jobs, they *attack* them – eager to make contributions. And the results are obvious: customers are delighted, employees are energized, innovations – large and small – happen with regularity, revenues are healthy, and the organization continually grows and develops.

Consider this: Your success – your very job itself – depends upon motivation! It's a critical component of leadership ... something deserving of your constant attention and focus. Fact is, if you can't open the door of possibility for others, or light a fire under someone to create a sense of importance, the results you achieve will be mediocre at best. So, too, will be your reputation as a leader.

So how can you motivate people? Well, the academic answer is *you can't!* Motivation is internal – it comes from deep within each of us. The only person who can truly motivate a person *is* the person. Sure, you can order someone to do something. Pick up the proverbial stick and most people will comply. But that approach neither brings out a person's best effort, nor does it encourage sustained good performance. You don't have to be a rocket scientist to know that "my way or the highway" supervision is the anti-matter of enthusiasm and commitment.

Although you can't control motivation, you certainly can *affect* it. You can create conditions where employees want to be motivated and therefore motivate themselves. And here's one you can take to the bank: With few exceptions, all people want to achieve, contribute, and be a part of something special. Our inherent drive challenges us to achieve. The task of the leader, then, is to harness and nurture that drive; to feed it and encourage it to grow. The following pages should help you do just that.

Motivation Tips

■ **Teach Business Literacy**
One powerful way to get people motivated is to teach them the business of the business. The more people understand how a successful organization is run, the better they'll be able to contribute to your overall mission and the bottom line … and feel like they truly are a part of your success.

■ **Involve Them In Decision Making**
Have an important decision to make? Let employees decide! Or at least ask for their ideas and suggestions. They are, after all, the ones who will feel the impact the most. Besides, you'll probably end up with a better decision – one that your people will be inclined to support because they helped make it.

■ **Let Your Employees Lead**
Help others on your team develop by letting them take the lead on certain activities and projects. Most of us like "being in charge" – at least some of the time. It's a great way to build skills, commitment, and responsibility.

■ **Address Performance Problems Early**
One of the surest ways to *de*motivate employees is allowing people to do sub-par work. When that happens, others have to pick up the slack. You owe it to the rest of the team to address an employee's deficiencies as soon as you become aware of them. Waiting only increases the intensity of everyone else's bad feelings.

■ **"Spread The Wealth"**
Rotate the drudge work so that everyone shares part of the load. Likewise, spread around the high-profile assignments so that every person has an occasional opportunity to strut his or her stuff.

■ **Keep Them Informed**
Hold regular "state of the business" meetings to keep everyone informed on what's happening within the organization (future plans, new products or services, planned purchases, etc.). Make sure people do NOT feel "kept in the dark."

Go Beyond The Tangible

To be sure, tangible acknowledgments (awards) for long-term service and special accomplishments certainly have their place. But lasting motivation occurs when people are given challenging assignments, fulfilling tasks, and ongoing, positive feedback. Put your focus there, and you'll cause people to care about themselves AND the job they're doing.

If you ask people confidentially what they want most in their job – if they're paid anything decent at all – they will say a greater sense of self-worth …
~ Fritz Maytag

Think "Development"

Make developing the members of your team (and yourself) one of your top priorities. Besides providing formal training, pursue opportunities for building skills, awareness, and confidence that require minimal time and resources (e.g., watching videos, distributing industry publications, mentoring, etc.).

Always Give The "Why"

A combined lesson from Human Nature 101 and Common Sense 101: There's a much better chance that people will be motivated and give their enthusiastic support if they understand the *reason* behind a goal, assignment, or decision. So, always follow the *what* with the *why*!

Respect *Their* Time

If you expect employees to believe that their work is important, you have to believe it, too. More importantly, you have to *behave* like you believe it! Don't expect people to drop whatever they're doing every time you need something. Instead, ask if they have a few minutes to chat. Better yet, ask for a time when they'll be available to meet with you.

Self-Assessment On Motivation

The key to sparking employee motivation is turning your good intentions into actions. You have to *apply* the ideas and strategies you find in this handbook, as well as others you discover ... you have to *"walk* the motivation talk." And to make sure you stay on track, you should monitor and periodically assess how well you're doing. Here's a short self-assessment to help you do that.

Mark your calendar or personal planner as a reminder. Once every three months, get a notepad, turn to this page, and answer the questions below. Analyze your responses. Are you satisfied with what you see? If you are, keep doing what you've been doing. If you're not satisfied, make the appropriate changes. It is, after all, *your* success that's ultimately at stake!

What SPECIFICALLY have I done in the last 3 months to ...

... Help others learn, develop, and grow?

... Support the people who work for, and with, me?

... Communicate, listen, and keep people informed?

... Involve people in the processes, decisions, and changes that affect them?

... Recognize performance and reward achievement?

... Create and encourage fun and enjoyment?

... Maintain high standards and expectations?

... Exhibit contagious enthusiasm?

... Demonstrate that I care – about work AND people?

... Set the example for the behaviors I desire from others?

from *180 Ways To Walk The Motivation Talk*

How To ...

Build A Reputation As An Effective Communicator

Know what activity you engage in the most as a leader? It's communicating! Combine all the time you spend making and returning phone calls, sending and responding to e-mails, writing notes, memos, and reports, meeting with co-workers, customers, and vendors, making presentations, and the like, and you'll probably find that 70-90% of your total working hours involve some form of communication – **all for the ultimate purpose of building "USA": Understanding, Support, and Acceptance.**

Truth be told, you don't just engage in communication – you *rely* on it. It's *what* you use to inform, instruct, direct, develop, motivate, convince, correct, collaborate, and achieve; it's *how* you affect performance, build trust, and shape an environment of business partnership. And since the majority of what you do involves communication, the majority of your success (and your reputation) will be built around how well you do it.

Obviously, "communication" is a very broad topic – one that can't possibly be covered in depth with the pages available in this handbook. But you will find several proven and practical strategies you can immediately apply to enhance your overall effectiveness. And because *listening* is such a critical part of the communication process, it's been broken out into its own chapter (pages 17-20).

> *The art of communication is the language of leadership.*
> *~ James Humes*

Keys To Building
Understanding, Support, and Acceptance

Informal, Positive, and "User Friendly" Language
The style and tone of your communications are messages in and of themselves. Remember that simplicity shapes the understanding ... tone shapes the reaction.

Multiple Communications In Different Forms
Frequency and diversity can increase communication effectiveness. Two basic rules of thumb: 1) The more frequent the exposure, the greater the anticipation and likelihood of acceptance; 2) The more diverse the format of successive communications, the greater the impact and retention.

A "What's In It For You" Approach
Nothing fosters support and acceptance better than personal benefit. Emphasize how the plan, policy, decision, etc., will benefit various employee groups and you'll increase your support base. Look for ways to make the underlying message of your communication be "This process is for you!"

Involvement and Participation
Employees tend to support what they (and their peers) help create. So look for opportunities to involve employees in communication development and delivery such as providing quotes and anecdotes, helping develop visuals, offering content input, proofing, assisting in presentations, providing feedback on communications *before* they're issued, etc.

Realism
Most people are turned-off by what they perceive as unrealistic claims, goals, and promises. There are no "cure-all's" in the world ... and your employees know it. When it comes to communicating your messages, be positive and upbeat – tell it like you see it ... just don't over "sell" it.

Communication Tips

■ Watch Your Language
Try to avoid: technical terms and acronyms that the entire audience may not understand, "fifty-cent words" thrown in to make you sound smart, and ambiguous words (*frequently, rarely, a lot,* etc.) that often have different meanings to different people.

■ Use *Fewer* Words
After writing a letter, memo, presentation script, etc., edit it with the goal of eliminating 15-20% of the words. It's not hard to find unnecessary wording if you really look for it.

■ Avoid "Data Dumps"
Narrow communications down to no more than three key points. Bombard people with more information than they can handle (or remember) and they'll tune-out.

■ Use Visual Messages
Try communicating creatively by using stories, examples, pictures, props, etc., to convey your message and increase retention.

■ Get Feedback From Your Staff
Have employees critique your communication skills. Ask everyone to respond (anonymously), in writing, to the following question: "What two to three things can I do to be a more effective communicator?" Thank people for their willingness to provide you with input. And make sure you ACT on the information you receive.

And the next page contains tips for specific forms of communication ...

When Using E-mail ...
- Use the "subject" line to inform ("Meeting changed to April 5") rather than merely identify the topic ("Meeting change"). You'll increase the odds that people will pay attention.
- Don't over-use "urgent." People will ignore it if used too often.
- Be careful what you include – your message might be forwarded to others.

When Writing ...
- State your objective in the first paragraph. Don't make people sift through reams of paper to get to your purpose.
- Write like you speak. Imagine you're having a conversation. What would you say to communicate your point? Write *that* down on paper.
- Whenever possible, limit your document to one page. This will force you to "cut to the chase" – something your readers will greatly appreciate.

When Leaving Voice Mails ...
- Give the date and time of your call ... and your name. Don't assume people will recognize your voice.
- Immediately describe the purpose of the call.
- Keep it to one issue per voice message. If you have more than one point to cover, you're probably better off talking "live."

When Presenting ...
- Start on time ... and *stay* on time.
- Begin with a description of what you'll cover – end with a summary and a review of any next steps.
- Supply the notes (handouts) so people can focus on your message.

How well we communicate is determined not by how well we say things, but how well we are understood.
~ Andrew Grove

How To ...

Hire And Promote Right, So You Can Manage With Ease

"You can pay in the beginning, or you can pay in the end ... with interest!" There's great truth in that old saying – and its relevance to management comes through loud and clear when you look at the functions of hiring and promoting.

One (of many) things that all managers have in common is the desire to fill new or vacant positions with good people. What isn't all that common, however, is the amount of effort and energy devoted to selection processes. Hey, we're all busy. Of course we need to fill slots. Sure "staffing" is important. But our platters are usually full. And the temptation is great to rush through hiring and promoting activities rather than taking the time and following the steps necessary to identify the best people for the jobs. That's no problem if you're blessed with a lion's share of luck and good fortune. But if you're like the rest of us, there's a good chance that, down the road, you'll end up spending a ton of headache-producing time trying to fix the people problems that typically result from rushed selections.

In most cases, the *more* effort you put into hiring and promoting, the *less* effort you need to devote to managing the performance of the people you bring on. The trade-offs are obvious ... the choices are yours. And *you* have to live with (and deal with) the results of your choices.

Undoubtedly, your organization has established selection procedures you'll need to follow. What we've done, in the next several pages, is provide ideas and strategies to augment your specific processes – to help you hire the best, brightest, and most productive people.

Selection Tips

■ Draw A Line In The Dirt ...
… and stop hiring (and promoting) individuals who don't clearly demonstrate their beliefs and behaviors regarding values such as integrity, respect,
responsibility, etc. Don't fall into the "belief trap" that you can train for these
characteristics at some later date. It rarely happens!

■ Hire People For *Who* They Are
One of the biggest mistakes most employers make is to value previous experience above all else. In today's rapidly changing world, however, experience is "how it *used* to be done." Whenever possible, hire people for traits
like hard-working, good team players, integrity, etc. – rather than just the
skills they've acquired from past experiences.

■ Remember: To Get The Best, You Have To TEST
The most reliable predictor of success on the job is not experience, education, or age. The best predictor is testing. Test for every important criterion
in the job requirements.

■ Hire For *Tomorrow's* Job
Don't just hire for a position, hire for the future. Jobs, technologies, and
markets are changing faster than ever. Hire people who are intelligent, quick
learners, and adaptable to change.

■ Use Targeted *Team* Interviews
Have multiple interviewers each focus on evaluating different applicant
factors and characteristics. Divi-up things like work history, technical skills,
teamwork, enthusiasm, honesty, and ethics among the interviewer group.

**The most expensive person you'll ever hire
is the one you end up having to fire.
So hire tough ... HIRE RIGHT!**

■ Bring On People Who Are *Different* From You
You don't need anyone else to think what you think and do what you do.
You're already there! Look for fresh and different people who will bring fresh
and different ideas. Hire for diversity.

Try A "Four Question Interview"

First, to get an overview of an applicant's history, say something like:
Tell me about your very first paying job and three things you learned from it.
Most people will respond with some kind of part-time work during their
school years. This gives you a glimpse into their work ethic and motivation.
Then have the applicant tell you a little about each successive job and what
was learned.

Second, for every trait, skill, or characteristic that is important to success
in the job you're filling, say: *On a scale of one to ten, rank yourself in terms
of* [e.g., communication skills] *and please explain your reasoning.*

Third: *How were you rated in the areas we've just discussed on your last
performance appraisal? Could you mail or fax me a copy of the last one you
received?*

Fourth: *Is there anything else you'd like to tell me about yourself and your
abilities before I answer any questions you have?*

from *180 Ways To Build A Magnetic Culture*

■ Rate The Answers, Not The Applicant
If you conclude the interview feeling that you like the person and want to
make an offer, go over your notes and pretend that a person you don't like
gave you the same answers to a few questions. Are they still good answers?

■ Keep Your Ears Open For "We's"
Listen for the "we" word ... unless you're looking for an "I" person. One
trait of good team players – no matter their level or function – is the use of
the word "we" when describing previous work situations and achievements.

■ Think Long Term

Never take a hiring or promotion decision lightly. Who you hire today will determine what your organization will be tomorrow.

■ Keep It Legal

The last thing you need is a lawsuit. The easiest way to determine whether what you want to ask is discriminatory is to ask yourself if the question is directly related to the person's ability to do the job. Race, religion, national origin, marital status, age, disability, Workers' Compensation, and injury information are all protected. Whether or not the person has children or dependents has no bearing on their ability to do the job. If your concern is dependability, ask: "How many times did you miss work this past year?" The safest and best route is to contact your HR department and request any available guidelines for interview procedures.

■ Don't Skip Background Checks

When thousands of applications were screened by a reference/background checking service, it was found that one in ten applicants screened had a criminal record; one in three misrepresented themselves on the application; and one in four provided false education and credential records. If it's not already a part of your employment process, get written authorization from all applicants to check their references and run background checks through reputable service providers.

■ Do Lunch

Take a candidate you're serious about to lunch and observe their personal traits and behaviors. Things like table manners, conversation in an informal setting, and treatment of wait staff can be very revealing.

■ Do A "Post Mortem"

Each time you conclude your hiring activities, gather all involved staff and evaluate the process. How pleased are you with the overall outcome? What worked well? What didn't? What can you do to make the process just ten percent better the next time? Consider asking new hires for their input. And once you've collected this information, ACT ON IT!

How To ...

Listen Your Way To Improved Trust And Understanding

If you were asked "Who taught you how to speak, read, and write?" you'd probably be able to list a whole series of people who helped you develop those important and much used communication skills. But what if the question was: "Who taught you how to listen?" If you're like most people, the answer would be "no one." That's truly ironic because, on average, listening is the part of communication we engage in the most (40% listening, 35% speaking, 16% reading, 9% writing), and it's the one for which we typically receive the least training. Therefore, it's the form of communication that most of us are least proficient at ... a critical leadership skill that far too often is ignored.

So why do we pay so little attention to listening? Two reasons: 1) We assume that because we hear well, we also listen well. But that just isn't true. Hearing is the mechanical (physiological) function of receiving sounds. Listening, however, is an interpretive function which involves turning those sounds into meaning. The two are very different. 2) We see listening as a passive rather than active activity. And in today's fast-pace, quick-fix, take charge business environment, being passive is viewed as being weak. But wrong again! Effective listening is an *active* process that requires skill, discipline, and practice.

Put forth the effort to be an effective listener and you'll:

- Minimize misunderstanding, assumptions, and mistakes;
- Reduce the time you'll need to spend solving problems;
- Increase trust, cooperation, loyalty, and commitment;
- Decrease stress, tension, and bad feelings;
- Eliminate "I had no idea that was happening" surprises; and
- Build more positive working relationships.

Active Listening

Effective listening is an active process that requires attention and focus. It's important that you concentrate on the words and behaviors of the speaker – without passing immediate judgement. There will be plenty of time for evaluation of the message down the road. The key, here, is remembering that the goal of listening is UNDERSTANDING – "I want to hear what you have to say" … "I want to know what you are thinking and feeling" … "I want to understand what the world looks like through your eyes." You don't have to agree with a person's position in order to understand where they're coming from and why they feel as they do. And once you have that knowledge, you'll be better able to work constructively with the employee and establish a mutually beneficial relationship of success.

Listening is also a demonstration of respect. When you listen to others, you're non-verbally saying: "Your thoughts and ideas are important" … "Your concerns are important" … "YOU are important." The opposite is also true: Failing to listen is a sign of *dis*respect. That's why you need to recognize and then minimize those behaviors that get in the way of true understanding.

COMMON ROADBLOCKS TO LISTENING

(Put a check mark next to any you've been guilty of in the past … and need to work on in the future)

☐ Allowing distractions (interruptions, phone calls, pagers, papers on your desk, daydreaming, etc.) to take your focus away from the speaker.

☐ Lack of adequate time and/or impatience with the speaker's inability to express his or her thoughts clearly and quickly.

☐ Thinking about what you'll say next rather than what the speaker is saying now.

☐ Interrupting, finishing the speaker's sentences, and overall "tuning out" because you assume you already know what the person has to say.

☐ Immediately disagreeing with the person's position and then allowing your beliefs and emotions to overpower the conversation.

☐ Feeling the need for "immediate closure" – moving too quickly to telling, convincing, instructing, correcting, solving, or whatever other action you feel is necessary to "put this issue to rest, now."

Listening Tips

■ Remind Yourself Of Your Goal
Before talking with another person, write "My goal is to UNDERSTAND!" on a piece of paper. Keep that paper in front of you and glance at it periodically.

■ Minimize Distractions
Whenever possible, pick a place to talk that's free from distractions. Turn off your phone or pager. Let others know you don't want to be disturbed. If bad listening conditions cannot be corrected, adjust quickly with concentration – or pick another place and time.

■ Give Your *Total* Attention
Establish and maintain eye contact with the speaker. Concentrate on the words he or she is saying … and the overall message they're conveying. Pretend that you'll be tested on everything the person says.

■ *Show* That You're Listening
Lean forward, unfold your arms, nod your head, and respond to what is said with an occasional "Okay," "I see," "Uh Huh," "I understand," etc.

PARAPHRASING

Unquestionably, the best technique for effective listening is paraphrasing: repeating, in your own words, what someone says – to *their* satisfaction. Example: "Kim, let me make sure I understand. You're saying that …. Is that correct?"

Paraphrasing provides two distinct benefits. First, it helps ensure understanding. It just may be that what you heard is not what the person meant. Paraphrasing allows him or her to respond with either "Yes, that's what I'm saying," or "No, that's not right. What I'm saying is …." If it's the latter, you have an immediate opportunity for clarification. Second, paraphrasing is another way to show the person that you *are* listening and are making a sincere effort to get their message. That's reassuring; it helps eliminate tension and provides an incentive for the person to continue sharing their thoughts and feelings.

■ Focus On Content, Not Delivery
Remember that some people are more articulate than others. Some have difficulty expressing themselves – they may be awkward with phrases, they may misuse words, or they may take a long time to communicate simple ideas. Don't get hung up on their presentation. Assume they're doing the best they can, and look for every opportunity to be supportive and demonstrate patience. Just don't speak *for* them.

■ NEVER Interrupt!
Interrupting – including finishing a person's sentences – is disrespectful, frustrating, and counterproductive to effective communication.

Ask Questions For Clarification ... And Encouragement

If the person says something you don't understand, ask for clarification in a non-challenging way. Saying things like "Scott, I'm not sure I really understand what you're saying. Could you go over that again?" or "How do you see that working?" or "I'm not all that familiar with what happened. Can you fill me in a little?" not only fosters clarity and understanding, but also encourages the speaker to keep talking.

■ Reflect On Non-Verbal Communication
Pay attention to the speaker's body language. Does he or she seem nervous? Angry? Scared? Reflect on their feelings: "Miguel, I'm sensing that this is really disturbing for you. Can you tell me what you're feeling right now?" Addressing non-verbal communication can help draw out issues that might otherwise be left unspoken and unaddressed. And, they can help separate *apparent* messages and concerns from *real*, underlying ones.

How To ...

Make The Most Of Your Time – And Your Meetings

So many responsibilities ... so little time? Can you relate? Most leaders can. It's no secret that our economy has changed dramatically. And business organizations have responded with their own brand of dramatic change. Leaner workforces, flatter organizational charts, and larger spans of control are the order of the day. "Do more with less" is the new battle cry. And the demands placed on leaders' time has continually increased.

Yes, the demands have increased, but the time available to meet those demands hasn't. There's still only twenty-four hours per day, seven days per week, fifty-two weeks per year. That's why managing your time more effectively (a.k.a. "working smarter") is more important than ever before.

Ever notice that, while everyone has the same number of minutes each day, some people regularly seem to get more done than you? You may have wondered what they have that you don't. The answer is NOTHING! You see, it's not what they *have*, it's what they *know*. They know how to use time wisely. And you can, too.

The good news is that making more efficient use of your time isn't all that difficult. It just requires that you move away from the things that waste your time ... and move toward the things that maximize it. Mixing a few solid strategies with a bunch of self-discipline will get you there. The following pages supply the strategies – the self-discipline is up to you. And here's a guarantee: The results will definitely be worth the effort!

Learn to manage your time and you'll be more productive and successful. You'll likely reduce your stress and fatigue levels. And, you'll be a better leader.

Time Management Tips

■ Prioritize Your Work

Tasks are commonly categorized in terms of: 1) "importance" – the level to which they add value to customers and the organization, or contribute to the accomplishment of significant goals, and 2) "urgency" – the assigned or perceived speed of required completion. Here's how to determine priorities:

> HIGH priority: important and urgent tasks
> MEDIUM priority: important but not urgent tasks
> LOW priority: urgent but not important tasks

Have a task that's not important and not urgent? Faghetaboutit! Try your very best to work on the highest priority tasks first.

■ Use Accomplishment-Oriented "To Do" Lists

Write down all the things you need to accomplish each day. Next to each item, write the time you feel it will take to complete it (be realistic in your estimates). Then, prioritize your list using the information in the previous tip. Next, add up the estimated times for completion. Based on the time total, remove or add lower priority items until your list is doable. Finally, WORK THE LIST – checking-off items as you complete them. Work on developing the self-discipline that "with the exception of unexpected emergencies (or significant opportunities), if it's not on the list, I won't allow myself to get side-tracked with it."

■ Delegate

Are you regularly involved in activities that your employees could handle just as well? Do you occasionally do things that don't need to be done by some-one at your level? If so, you need to delegate more. Whatever time you need to spend preparing people to learn new tasks will pay dividends down the road in terms of saved time … and reduced stress. And, you'll be helping your people develop and grow.

■ Control Your Phone

Set specified times for returning phone calls. Give others preferred times for calling you. Identify times for working on important tasks where you rely on voice mail rather than answering calls. And when you do answer the phone, let people know how much time you have available … and stick to it!

Maximize E-Mail
Consider using e-mail as your primary source of communication. You can respond at times that are convenient for you. Just make sure you get back to people within a reasonable time frame and that you periodically check for high-priority items that have come in.

Learn To Say "No" ... Tactfully
Hey, it's great to pitch in and help other people. But if it gets to the point where you're not getting *your* work done because you're doing someone else's, you have a problem. When you can't help someone, tell them so, give them the reason, and suggest alternative assistance ... or an alternative time when you will be available.

Go On An "In-Office Vacation"
Isolate yourself in order to work on critical projects and ask others to handle issues as if you really were gone. Clear it with your boss and ask for his or her cooperation in honoring your "time off." And make sure that *you* act as if you aren't there (no phone calls, no socializing, etc.).

TARGET THE "TIME WASTERS"

Work with employees to identify inefficient uses of time that occur within your work unit. Select the three most significant items and develop a joint strategy for eliminating or minimizing them.

By the way, don't be surprised if "meetings" makes the list – it usually does. The first step toward more effective meetings is NOT to have them, if ...
... you're not prepared or have incomplete information;
... there's no real need for group interaction;
... people who need to be there can't make it;
... there's a cheaper yet equally effective way to accomplish the objective (e-mail, conference call, memo, etc.).

Convinced you DO need a meeting? Use the information on the next page to help make the event as effective as possible.

Six Steps To More Effective Meetings

1 Figure Out The Objective(s) First
Write a short, specific description of what you need to accomplish.
Example: "Review the fifteen action plans developed by the team and decide on those that will be implemented in the first quarter."

2 Plan The Event
Based on the objective(s) to accomplish, determine who needs to attend, what resources (information, equipment, etc.) you'll need, where and when the meeting will be held, when it will end, and what activities (brainstorming, small group assignments, etc.) you'll use.

3 Prepare The People
Distribute a detailed meeting Agenda to all participants 2-3 days in advance. Include the objective(s), administrative details (time, place, etc.), a list of who will attend, how participants should prepare and what they should bring.

4 Open With The Purpose, The Process, and The Ground Rules
Begin promptly. Thank everyone for their time. Review the agenda – including the objective(s), administrative details, and planned activities – and any "ground rules" (no side conversations, cell phones and pagers off, no leaving the room until assigned breaks, etc.).

5 Manage The Meeting
Maintain strict adherence to the agenda and time frames. Keep the group on track and encourage everyone to participate. Periodically summarize what's been accomplished so far. And keep the environment safe by minimizing criticism as well as distracting, counterproductive behaviors.

6 Close With A Review ... And A "Thank You"
Save the last ten minutes of every meeting for a summary of what took place and what actions will follow. Review the issues discussed, any questions or concerns that surfaced, the decisions made, the action plans that were developed (who will do what by when), and any follow up activities identified (the notes will be typed and distributed, we'll meet again on ____, etc.).

Finally, thank the attendees for their time, their participation, and their contributions.

How To ...

Eliminate The Nightmares Of Employee Performance Problems

Roll up your sleeves ... this is the tough part of leadership. Even in the very best organizations, managers will have to occasionally deal with a problem employee – uncooperative, chronically late, "just getting by" performance, etc.

Unsatisfactory performers (a.k.a. "Falling Stars") represent only a small percent of any team. Yet many managers spend an inordinate amount of their time with people in this group. And when that happens, the good and dependable majority of employees are shorted – failing to receive the attention they need and want. Spending so much time toiling over performance problems doesn't do a whole lot for *your* job satisfaction either.

Most managers are not comfortable addressing employee performance problems. That's easily understood. Performance issues are stressful, and many of us don't have the training and experience we need to deal with them. Nevertheless, there *will* be problems staring you square in the face. You can close your eyes, live with the situations, and accept the negative impact of performance deficiencies. Or, you can conduct performance improvement sessions in which employees will either commit to your standards – or choose to ignore the problem and face the logical consequences. The pages that follow will help you make those discussions more effective and help you achieve ...

The Two Goals of Managing Performance Problems

1. SOLVE THE PROBLEM, *and*

2. MAINTAIN THE RELATIONSHIP

Performance Improvement Session

The objectives of the performance improvement session are to describe the problem, gain the employee's agreement to solve it, and identify a solution that conforms to your expectations – and that will result in the employee changing his or her behavior. To achieve that, follow the steps listed below.

(For example purposes, a tardiness problem is presented. You should insert the appropriate information to match whatever issue you will be addressing.)

1. EXPLAIN WHY YOU CALLED THE MEETING – IDENTIFY THE PERFORMANCE PROBLEM AND ITS IMPACT ON OTHERS

"I called you in because there's a problem that needs to be addressed right away. The attendance standard for our work group is to be at work, every day, on time. But in the last week, you've been over ten-minutes late three times.

When you arrive late, customers have to wait to be helped and your co-workers have to rush around and pick up the slack for you."

2. ASK FOR THE EMPLOYEE'S AGREEMENT TO SOLVE THE PROBLEM

"Because starting on time is so important, I need your agreement to solve this problem and get your attendance back on track. Will you agree to correct this problem immediately?"

If the employee does not agree, re-emphasize the impact on others. If you've reviewed the problem and the impact a few times, but the employee still fails to agree, you'll need to discuss consequences (Step 3). If the employee does agree, proceed to Step 4.

3. REVIEW THE CONSEQUENCES THE EMPLOYEE WILL FACE IF THE PROBLEM CONTINUES

"What do you think will happen if this problem continues?" (Allow the employee to respond. Then agree with, correct, or expand on what he or she says. If they don't know, be prepared to clearly state the consequences.)

"I can't allow anyone to be habitually late because of the impact on the team and our clients. If this behavior continues, my next step will be to initiate formal discipline. I don't want that to happen, and I don't think you do either. But it is your choice."

4. REQUEST AN ACTION PLAN FROM THE EMPLOYEE

"So, specifically, what are you going to do to solve the problem and make sure we do not have this discussion again?"

Allow the person to come up with his or her own course of action, but be prepared to help with suggestions. Some solutions will be fairly simple, like "I'll reset my alarm clock and leave twenty minutes earlier." But occasionally, the employee may need a little time to develop a plan. That's okay. Just schedule another meeting, later that day, to discuss it – after he or she has had sufficient time to sort through the issue. After the person identifies a viable solution ...

5. REINFORCE THE EMPLOYEE'S COMMITMENT AND THEN CLOSE

"Good. This is a serious issue that requires your immediate attention. I expect that you'll solve this problem and begin arriving at work, on time, every day – starting tomorrow. Do we have an agreement? (Wait for response) *Thanks. I want you to know that I'm counting on you. I know you can do this."*

6. IMMEDIATELY FOLLOW UP BY GIVING THE EMPLOYEE A WRITTEN SUMMARY OF BOTH THE SESSION AND HIS OR HER ACTION PLAN

If the employee corrects the problem, recognize him or her for the success. If he or she doesn't follow through on their commitment, you'll need to consider more serious steps in the disciplinary process. And eventually you may have to let the person go. That's the toughest thing a leader ever has to do – even though it's just implementing the consequences of the person's chosen behavior.

Keys To Effective Performance Improvement Sessions

Preparation
Do your homework and collect all the relevant data before meeting with the employee. Do *not* base your discussion on secondhand information or assumptions. Get the facts.

Focusing on the problem behavior – not the employee
The problem is a behavioral issue, not a personal issue. Your conversation should be about bad performance, not a bad person.

Involving the employee in the discussion
Don't talk *at* the person, talk *with* him or her. Employees will commit to solutions THEY create far more quickly than ones that are dictated by you. After all, it is the *employee's* responsibility to solve the problem. He or she should do at least 50% of the talking … and you should do at least 50% of the listening!

Being crystal clear
You're dealing with a serious issue that requires change. Be direct and specific. Avoid talking in generalities – especially when discussing the consequences. You owe it to the person to "tell it like it is." Just make sure you do it constructively.

How To ...

Lead For "Dynamite" Customer Service

Ever stop to really think about what business you're in? Ask people, and they'll typically say things like: manufacturing, sales, healthcare, banking, insurance, computer software, food service, hospitality, retail, etc. If those are the kind of answers your employees would give, they'd be only *half* right!

Here's a one-question test: If all of your customers went away for good, would you still have a business ... *would your employees still have jobs?* Of course not! Well, that's your clue to the more important half of what they do: THEY'RE IN THE CUSTOMER SERVICE BUSINESS. And that means they not only need to know the right way to fix equipment, write programs, conduct a test, or whatever, they also need to know the right way to serve customers. Everyone needs to know it, and more importantly, everyone needs to *practice* it. And the leadership you provide plays a huge role in making that happen.

It seems that everywhere you look you find businesses proudly touting statements like: "Customers come first," "We're here to serve," and "We go the extra mile." And the irony is that while all this noble, well-intended talk is on the rise, it's apparent that the quality of service, in general, is on a steady decline. Organizations are losing business every day because their people aren't providing the level of service that customers demand and deserve.

By applying the ideas presented on the following pages – by focusing on the people who focus on the customers – you can help ensure that you don't end up as one of the losers. Pay attention and apply what you read. You owe it to your customers, you owe it to your organization, and you owe it to yourself.

Customer Service Leadership Tips

■ Start With Hiring

Make your selection process part of your overall customer service strategy. During interviews, ask questions like: "If you get this job, describe the kinds of things you will do to provide superior customer service." Also, pose hypothetical customer service situations and ask candidates to describe how they would handle them.

■ Include It In Job Descriptions

Make "Customer Service" a part of ALL written or verbal job descriptions – no matter the function or level. In hiring interviews, orientation, and on-the-job training, emphasize that *everyone* is in the customer service business. And make sure that each employee understands how he or she directly (or indirectly) "touches" the customer.

INTERESTING TIDBIT

Of customers who take their business somewhere else:
15% find *cheaper* products elsewhere
15% find *better* products elsewhere
65% leave because of poor customer service

The Forum Corporation

■ *EX*pect It

Clarify your expectations about customer service. Condense them to 3-5 key principles, give them a label (e.g., "The Big Four" or "The Game Plan"), and communicate them to everyone. Then, have follow-up meetings with individual employees to ensure that they know what is expected of them.

■ *IN*spect It

Remember that people do what's *ex*pected when it's *in*spected! So include "Customer Service" feedback in all performance evaluations. Prior to conducting evaluations, ask employees to submit a list of the specific things they've done to help provide superior customer service.

■ Make Them Experts
Help your employees become experts on the products and services you offer. Give them manuals and marketing brochures; have them talk with product developers, vendors, and service deliverers; encourage employees to use the products and services themselves. The more they know, the better their service will be.

■ Don't Forget Your Internal Customers
Do your people provide services for other departments, groups, or individual employees *within* your organization? If so, those people are customers too, and they deserve the same level of good service as the general public who does business with your organization. Make sure your people are tuned-in to this group.

Along that line ...

■ View *Employees* As Customers
Give your people the same respect and attention that you want them to give to the people that *they* serve. Satisfied employees tend to produce satisfied customers.

■ Walk Awhile In *Their* Shoes
Keep in touch with your customers and your employees by spending at least two hours each month working alongside customer service staff members.

■ Give Them "The Parameters"
Make sure your customer-contact employees know how much discretion they have (ability to discount or comp goods, services, shipping, etc.) when addressing customer complaints and problems. Encourage them to do whatever is necessary – within reasonable limits – to make customers happy without having to come to you, first, for permission.

■ Meet And Share
Have regular meetings among customer service reps to share experiences, techniques, and "best practices."

from *180 Ways To Walk The Customer Service Talk*

■ Make It Matter
Make sure there are positive consequences for people who provide good service and appropriate negative consequences for those who willfully fail to meet your service standards.

■ Look For Paralyzing Policies
Ask employees to identify policies and procedures that get in the way of providing good service. Then do your best to update, modify, or eliminate as many as you can.

■ Celebrate Successes
Make heroes of employees who provide exceptional customer service. Share their stories with others. This will motivate the entire team. Motivated employees tend to go above and beyond for your customers … and for the organization.

Motivate them, train them, care about them, and make winners out of them… we know that if we treat our employees correctly, they'll treat the customers right. And if customers are treated right, they'll come back.
~ J. Marriott, Jr.

How To ...

Recognize Your Way To Better Results

There's certainly no shortage of research and expert opinion on the positive impacts of recognition in the workplace. Studies continually show that recognition fosters job satisfaction, builds self-esteem, and reinforces desired performance. It supports quality, strengthens trust and loyalty, and helps shape a "magnetic" culture that attracts and keeps the very best people. Yet, despite these (and a lot more) widely accepted and well-documented benefits, too many recognition opportunities are being missed in too many organizations, every day.

Here's a short, two-question survey that you'll probably be able to answer without much thought:

1. Ever feel unappreciated or under-recognized for the good work you do?
2. Ever miss opportunities to recognize people reporting to you for the good work that *they* do?

If you're like most folks, there's a good chance your two answers were DUH! and OOPS! (a.k.a., yes and yes). Of course, all of us occasionally feel taken for granted. We know firsthand how lousy that feels. And when we fail to give recognition to our employees, we pass along that same lousy feeling. We do it not because we're bad people, but because we're human ... and we sometimes lose sight of what's truly important. But as a leader, you have an opportunity to change that. In fact, you have an *obligation* to change that. You owe it to your employees ... you owe it to your organization ... and considering the benefits to be gained, you owe it to yourself.

Recognition is about acknowledging good results and reinforcing positive performance; it's about shaping an environment in which contributions are noticed and appreciated. And that's a responsibility shared by ALL managers, supervisors, and team leaders.

Recognition Checklist

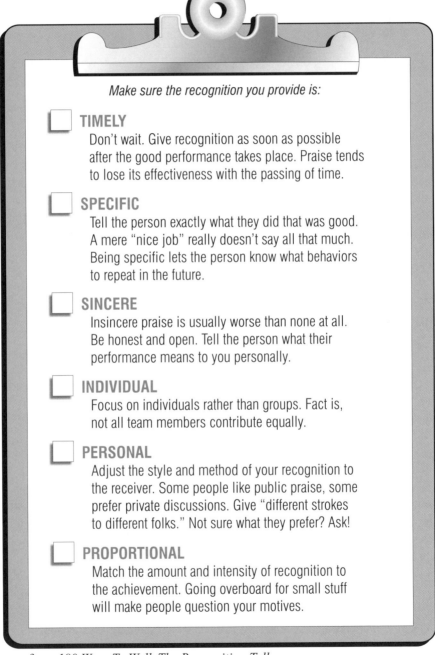

Make sure the recognition you provide is:

☐ **TIMELY**
Don't wait. Give recognition as soon as possible after the good performance takes place. Praise tends to lose its effectiveness with the passing of time.

☐ **SPECIFIC**
Tell the person exactly what they did that was good. A mere "nice job" really doesn't say all that much. Being specific lets the person know what behaviors to repeat in the future.

☐ **SINCERE**
Insincere praise is usually worse than none at all. Be honest and open. Tell the person what their performance means to you personally.

☐ **INDIVIDUAL**
Focus on individuals rather than groups. Fact is, not all team members contribute equally.

☐ **PERSONAL**
Adjust the style and method of your recognition to the receiver. Some people like public praise, some prefer private discussions. Give "different strokes to different folks." Not sure what they prefer? Ask!

☐ **PROPORTIONAL**
Match the amount and intensity of recognition to the achievement. Going overboard for small stuff will make people question your motives.

from *180 Ways To Walk The Recognition Talk*

Recognition Tips

■ Know Your Employees As People
Find out what's important to the people who report to you. Ask about hobbies, favorite sports, vacations, family, etc. This shows that you're interested in *who* they are in life as well as *what* they represent at work. That's recognition at its most basic level!

■ Work On Your Attitude
Develop an "attitude of gratitude" by creating a written list of performance and behaviors deserving of recognition. Jot down everything you can think of. Add to the list periodically. Most importantly, keep an eye out for people who do things on your list and recognize them! Here are 10 recognition opportunities to get your list started:

■ Long-term positive performance such as perfect attendance for a year.
■ Exceeding expectations, like coming in under budget.
■ Volunteering for a tough assignment.
■ Helping others in the organization meet *their* goals.
■ Displaying "contagious enthusiasm" on the job.
■ Submitting a cost-saving or time-saving idea.
■ Requesting/accepting additional responsibilities.
■ Going "above and beyond" for a customer.
■ Successful completion of an in-house training course or outside continuous education program.
■ Keeping a cool head under pressure.

■ Diversify!
Don't get in a rut giving the same kind of recognition all the time. Mix it up. Use a variety of verbal "atta boys," written commendations, awards, perks, etc. You'll make it more meaningful for the receivers and more fun for you!

■ Get In The Habit
We're all creatures of habit. Repeat an action enough times and it becomes habitual – an unconscious behavior. Here's a worthwhile habit to work on developing: Each day, "catch" at least one person doing something good ... and praise them. Over time, you'll acquire a natural tendency to focus on the good stuff!

■ Become A Recognition Catalyst
Once you find a person to recognize, pass the information on to a senior manager to add his or her personal message. With few exceptions, the person being recognized will appreciate acknowledgment from "Mr./Ms. Big." And the senior manager will no doubt appreciate the opportunity to recognize a valuable employee.

By Way Of Introduction ...

Seize every opportunity to introduce people in your work group to customers, visitors, vendors, "big wigs," etc. The message to employees: "You're important ... I want people to meet you." Pound for pound, introductions may be the most effective low-cost/high-impact recognition you can give.

■ Notify The Family
Send a letter or card to the person's family describing her/his performance and the positive impact it has on the organization. Close with something like: "We're very proud of Chris ... you should be, too."

■ Give 'Em A Card
Keep a supply of "Thanks for a Job Well Done" (or similar message) cards handy at all times so you can strike while the recognition iron is hot. Set a personal goal to give out as many well-deserved cards as possible during the next 12 months.

■ Ask Them What THEY Think
Recognize team members by asking for their ideas and input on work processes, future purchases, and decisions you are facing. The message: "Your opinions are valuable ... YOU are valuable."

■ Name Something In Their Honor
Officially dedicating "The Karen Jones Printer" or the "Bill Lee Forklift" by affixing an inexpensive engraved brass plaque can be a fun yet powerful form of recognition. And its impact will extend well beyond the presentation.

How To ...

Coach Your Way To A High-Performance Culture

Pull out a dictionary, look up the word *lead* and you'll find definitions like: "to show the way; to guide or direct; to serve as a route for; to influence the opinions and actions of others." Those definitions pretty much sum up your role when it comes to the performance of your people. As a leader, you're responsible for helping employees achieve, grow, and do their very best work. Your success is directly linked to their success. And their success is directly linked to your activities – namely your *coaching* activities.

Examine any workforce and you'll find three categories of employee performers:

"Falling Stars"   *"Middle Stars"*   *"Super Stars"*

1) "Falling Stars" – the small number with performance problems (as addressed on pages 25-28), 2) "Middle Stars" – the vast majority of solid, dependable employees, and 3) "Super Stars" – that small, but special, group of superior performers. People in all three categories need help maintaining and improving their performance levels. And that's where you come in.

You *can* influence how employees do their jobs. In fact, you MUST influence it. That's *your* job. So how do you do it? By being a good coach ... by applying the time-tested performance management strategies found on the following pages.

Coaching Tips (What Good Coaches DO)

Provide the TRAINING employees need

Start on day one with a thorough orientation, and then make training an ongoing activity. Work with each person to craft a personal development plan that includes a combination of structured training programs, OJT, mentoring by subject matter experts, and special assignments. And periodically ask your people to assess their own competency levels and identify training they feel they need to improve.

Let them know your EXPECTATIONS

People can't meet expectations if they don't know what they are – and they won't know unless they're told. Meet with each employee to discuss the performance requirements of their job and your expectations. Start with a list of their job duties and responsibilities. Review *what* they should do and *how well* they should do it. And clarify your expectations regarding quality, teamwork, customer service, etc.

Offer regular FEEDBACK on how they're doing

Avoid the common mistake of letting "annual reviews" be the only feedback employees receive. Let people know how they're doing on a regular basis. And make sure your feedback: 1) pinpoints observable actions and behaviors, 2) is given as soon as possible after the behavior takes place, and 3) focuses on the perform*ance* rather than the perform*er*.

"Coaching sets the pace to get the best out of others while giving the best of yourself."
~ David Cottrell

Remove any OBSTACLES they may be facing

Ask each member of your work group to identify the three most significant obstacles affecting their performance (e.g., faulty equipment, unclear instructions, prohibitive policies, etc.). Create a master list and start working to eliminate as many as you can.

 ### Work with them to set GOALS

Meet with your employees every 3, 6, or 12 months to identify the results they plan to accomplish during the next time period. Set up a monitoring schedule to see how they're progressing and to help them stay on track.

Help them learn from MISTAKES *and* SUCCESSES

When mistakes occur, sit down with employees to identify the key learning: "What can/will you do in the future to make sure that this error isn't repeated?" Do the same for successes. Besides congratulating employees for their achievements, ask them to pinpoint the actions and behaviors that led to their success. Encourage them to apply those same factors to future tasks and projects.

Provide REINFORCEMENT for the behaviors you want

When you recognize and reward good behavior, you increase the employee's motivation to keep doing it. Recognition is the single most-effective technique for building (and maintaining) desired performance. It's a proven management strategy … and a demonstration of true appreciation for good work. And because it's so important, we dedicated the previous chapter to it alone.

ELIMINATE PUNISHMENT for doing a good job

We ALL have a tendency to rely on our best people to get us through difficult situations. "You did such a great job handling that lousy situation, the next time we have one, we're giving it to you again." Sound familiar? Unless people really *want* all the tough stuff, being a victim of their own competence can be very de-motivating. So, spread the "tough stuff" around. Or at least make sure you make it worth people's while to take more than their fair share.

Don't Forget "The Super Stars"

Beware of the tendency to take superior performers for granted. They need your attention too. In fact, working with super stars (to help them stay that way) may provide the highest return on your coaching investment. Here are some tips for managing the people you rely on the most:

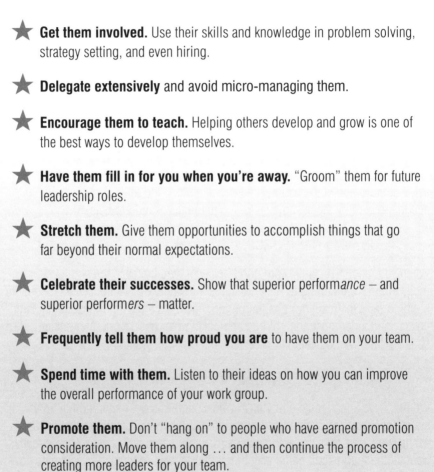

★ **Get them involved.** Use their skills and knowledge in problem solving, strategy setting, and even hiring.

★ **Delegate extensively** and avoid micro-managing them.

★ **Encourage them to teach.** Helping others develop and grow is one of the best ways to develop themselves.

★ **Have them fill in for you when you're away.** "Groom" them for future leadership roles.

★ **Stretch them.** Give them opportunities to accomplish things that go far beyond their normal expectations.

★ **Celebrate their successes.** Show that superior perform*ance* – and superior perform*ers* – matter.

★ **Frequently tell them how proud you are** to have them on your team.

★ **Spend time with them.** Listen to their ideas on how you can improve the overall performance of your work group.

★ **Promote them.** Don't "hang on" to people who have earned promotion consideration. Move them along ... and then continue the process of creating more leaders for your team.

from *The Manager's Coaching Handbook*

How To ...

Use Ethics And Values To Ensure Success

No book on leadership could be complete without addressing the most basic (and most important) management responsibility of all: Leading With Integrity. You meet that responsibility by making sure that your work group is *"about"* what your organization says *it* is "about." And in today's challenging business environment, doing that involves VALUES and it involves ETHICS. Both are critical to your success ... both are your ultimate competitive advantage.

Values and ethics represent the core of any organization. And all you have to do is read the newspaper or watch the evening news to know that they are more important, now, than ever before. We rely on them to ...

Provide direction and guidance for our decisions, our behaviors, and our day-to-day business practices;

Provide protection from improprieties that not only can destroy our standing and reputation, but also can expose us to legal liabilities;

Provide stability – solid anchors to hold on to in these unstable, ever-changing times;

Provide meaning and identity – the sense of who we are, what we do, and what we stand for that we all so desperately need.

Simply stated, values and ethics keep us *in* business and *out* of trouble. They help us attract and keep good customers ... and great employees. They are our guideposts – pointing the way to what's right and fair. And making sure that they "happen" truly is the highest priority for leaders at all levels.

Tips For Using Ethics And Values To Ensure Success:

■ Set The Example ...

... by checking your decisions and planned activities for "rightness" *before* implementing them. Answering "no" to one or more of the following would suggest the need for an alternative approach:

THE ETHICAL ACTION TEST

A. Is it legal?

B. Does it comply with our rules and guidelines?

C. Is it in sync with our organizational values?

D. Will I be comfortable and guilt-free if I do it?

E. Does it match our stated commitments and guarantees?

F. Would I do it to my family or friends?

G. Would I be perfectly okay with someone doing it to me?

H. Would the most ethical person I know do it?

from *Ethics4Everyone*

■ Keep Them "In Front Of People"

Make sure your organizational values and ethical standards are readily apparent and regularly communicated. Make ethics and values a regular topic of conversation. Add something about ethics (an article you read in a magazine or newspaper, a "best practice" from your organization, etc.) to the agenda of each staff meeting that you conduct. And periodically check your pulse by asking "How are we doing?" and by soliciting ideas on what the team can do more of, do less of, and do differently to make values and integrity-driven business practices your norm.

■ Review The Rules Of The Road

Don't assume that employees know all the laws and procedures that pertain to their jobs. MAKE SURE they know them! Give each person copies of all relevant guidelines, and review the information with them. Also provide updates as new information becomes available.

■ Provide Ethics And Values-Driven Education
Be sure that all training you provide (or send people to) not only teaches the mechanics of doing the job, but also provides the skills and information necessary to do the job according to your values and ethical standards. And try using hypothetical situations to address the ethical "gray areas" that employees may sometimes face.

■ Eliminate Offensive Words and Comments From Your Vocabulary
Simply put: Watch your mouth! Derogatory terms and off-color jokes have no place at work. They're degrading, unethical, and they can have legal repercussions. The words you use, the jokes you tell, and the e-mails you send say a lot more about *you* than the people you're referring to.

■ Accept A Few Wrong Turns
Let people know that mistakes can be made and careers can be built in spite of them – as long as the errors are infrequent, unintentional, and low in negative impact. When fear of failure is minimized, employees become less likely to engage in "cover-ups" which can lead to more serious problems. But if ethical violations are involved ...

■ Take Immediate Action
Respond quickly and thoroughly to ALL unethical behaviors. Take immediate steps to stop any inappropriate activity and correct the situation. Then, conduct an investigation – collecting all the facts. Finally, deal with the offender(s) according to your organizational procedures and guidelines. Demonstrate by *your* actions that you have zero tolerance for ethics violations.

Watch What You Measure

Employees tend to judge what's truly important by looking at what is monitored and measured – and what isn't. If you only track quantity, quality will be viewed as secondary; pay attention mostly to sales, and service will drop in priority. Take a moment to examine your "scorecards." Are you collecting data on *all* the things you say are important – or are you just zeroing-in on the bottom line ... and sending mixed messages?

■ Provide Places To Go
Make sure there are people within your organization to whom employees can turn for guidance and help with values-related issues – and for reporting suspected ethics violations. Look to establish alternative resources (more than just YOU) that employees trust and will use whenever the need is felt. And make sure everyone knows what assistance is available ... and how to access it.

■ Include Them In Your Performance Feedback
Build ethics and values into all performance discussions that you have with employees. Ask them for examples of ways they feel they've performed with integrity and supported your key values. Share *your* observations. Focus on "means" as well as "ends." And work with each person to develop a personal enhancement plan.

■ Include Them In Your Selection Process
Only hire and promote people who have demonstrated a commitment to business ethics and shared values. Make it known that *To work and advance here, you've got to be in sync with our values and perform with the highest integrity.*

WATCH OUT FOR "THE BIG FOUR":

GREED – The drive to acquire or possess more and more in one's self-interest;

SPEED – The motivation to cut corners in response to the "warp" pace of business;

LAZINESS – Taking the easy path of least effort and resistance;

HAZINESS – Acting and reacting without thinking.

These are the primary factors leading to unethical behavior. And they're all temptations that must be fought ... by everyone.

Closing Thoughts

Well, there you have it ... there you have *them* – "nuts and bolts" tips and techniques for effectively dealing with ten key areas of leadership.

Have we covered every aspect and responsibility of being a leader? Of course not. Have we provided everything there is to know about the ten subject areas addressed? No, again. We don't have the time to write a book that large, and you probably wouldn't have the time (or the desire) to read it.

What we have done is assemble a collection of proven strategies and practical "how to's" for what experience has taught us are important components of being an effective leader. Assuming that, like us, you have more things to do than time to do them, we've tried to zero-in on the information you need to not only survive, but also succeed in your vital leadership role.

But the strategies provided in this handbook are nothing more than good ideas. You have to put them into ACTION in order for their value and benefits to be realized.

So keep this book handy, re-read it periodically, refer to it often, and USE its contents to help you and your employees achieve the success you want and need.

✓ Please send me extra copies of: *Nuts'nBolts LEADERSHIP*

1-99 copies $9.95 each   100-499 copies $8.95 each   500+ copies please call

Nuts'nBolts Leadership	_____ copies X	_____	=$_____

Other Recommended Resources

WALK THE TALK® Leadership Development Library	_____ sets X	$ 99.95	=$_____
Leadership Courage	_____ copies X	$ 14.95	=$_____
Monday Morning Leadership	_____ copies X	$ 14.95	=$_____
180 Ways To Walk The Leadership Talk	_____ copies X	$ 9.95	=$_____
Listen UP, Leader!	_____ copies X	$ 9.95	=$_____

Product Total	$_____
*Shipping & Handling	$_____
Subtotal	$_____
Sales Tax:	
Texas Sales Tax – 8.25%	$_____
CA Sales/Use Tax	$_____
Total (U.S. Dollars Only)	$_____

(Sales & Use Tax Collected on TX & CA Customers Only)

*Shipping and Handling Charges

No. of Items	1-4	5-9	10-24	25-49	50-99	100-199	200+
Total Shipping	$6.75	$10.95	$17.95	$26.95	$48.95	$84.95	$89.95 + $0.25/book

Call 972.899.8300 for quote if outside continental U.S. Orders are shipped ground delivery 3-5 days. Next and 2nd business day delivery available – call 888.822.9255.

Name_____ Title_____

Organization_____

Shipping Address_____

City_____ (No P.O. Boxes) State_____ Zip _____

Phone_____ Fax_____

E-Mail_____

Charge Your Order: ❏ MasterCard   ❏ Visa   ❏ American Express

Credit Card Number_____ Exp. Date_____

❏ Check Enclosed (Payable to The WALK THE TALK Company)

❏ Please Invoice (**Orders over $250 ONLY**)   P.O. Number (required)_____

LKTHETALK.COM
ces for Personal and Professional Success

PHONE 888.822.9255 or 972.899.8300 M-F, 8:30-5:00 Cen.	**ONLINE** www.walkthetalk.com	**MAIL** WALK THE TALK Co. 1100 Parker Square, Suite 250 Flower Mound, TX 75028
	FAX 972.899.9291	

Prices effective December 2007 are subject to change.

The WALK THE TALK® Company

Since 1977, The WALK THE TALK® Company has helped individuals and organizations, worldwide, achieve success through Values-Based Practices. Our goal is both simple and straightforward: to provide you and your organization with high-impact resources for your personal and professional success!

We specialize in ...

- How-To Handbooks and Support Material
- Video Training Programs
- Inspirational Gift Books and Movies
- Do-It-Yourself Training Resources
- Motivational Newsletters
- 360° Feedback Processes
- The popular *212° the extra degree, Start Right...Stay Right,* and *Santa's Leadership Secrets®* Product Lines *and much more!*

To learn more call: 1.888.822.9255
E-mail: info@walkthetalk.com
Visit: www.walkthetalk.com

The Authors

Eric Harvey is a renowned author, consultant, speaker, and president of The WALK THE TALK® Company. His 30-plus years of professional experience are reflected in twenty-eight highly acclaimed books, including the best-selling *WALK THE TALK ... And Get The Results You Want* and *Ethics4Everyone* and *The Leadership Secrets of Santa Claus®*.

Paul Sims is a top-rated speaker, author, workshop facilitator, and senior consultant for The WALK THE TALK® Company. With over 30 years of business experience, Paul has built a solid reputation of getting positive results for client organizations of all types and sizes. He is co-author of WALK THE TALK publications, *Nuts'nBolts Leadership* and *Leading To Ethics*.